MORE GIGGLY RHYMES

Selected and illustrated by **Julie Park**

Put your
photograph
here
please

LITTLE MAMMOTH

George

YOUR PHOTO

I wish I had your photo
it'd be very nice
I would put it up in the attic
to scare away the mice.

MY FIRST PET

I won a goldfish at the fair,
But I don't think it's well.
It hasn't touched a scrap of food,
And it's begun to smell.

what a whiff!

It lays around the whole day long,
It's such a disappointment.
I'm taking it to see the vet,
To see if it needs ointment.

I've seen the vet, he says it's dead,
And I'm so very sad,
That goldfish was the very first,
Pet I have ever had.

I'm going to buy another one,
I liked it very much,
And anyway it's such a shame,
To waste that lovely hutch.

John Boon

Hands OFF
CAKE
THINK thin
What you eat to-day you wear tomorrow

GRANNY

My Granny's had her hair done
She's had it done bright red
She's had it dyed so it will hide
The grey bits in her head

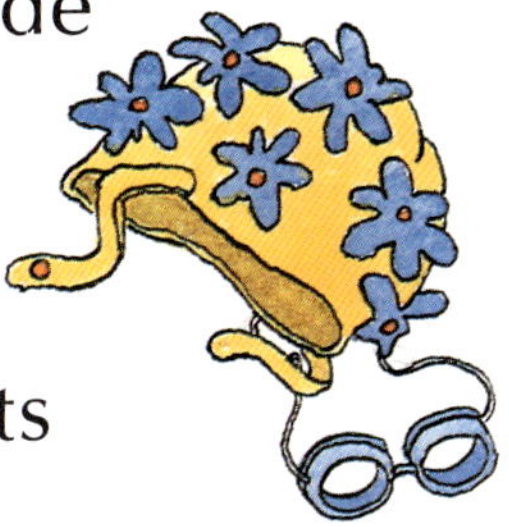

My Granny's started yoga
She wiggles on the floor
And ties herself up into knots
My Granny is no bore

My Granny's on a diet
She's stopped eating chips
And chocolate cakes and jammy buns
That put wobbles on her hips

My Granny's started swimming
She takes me to the pool
While I just flap she does front crawl
And makes me feel a fool

My Granny's really trendy
At the disco she's a wow
The problem is she seems to be
Much younger than me now!

Jill Batterley

I OFTEN MEET A MONSTER

I often meet a monster
While deep in sleep at night;
And I confess to some distress.
It gives me quite a fright.
But then again I wonder.
I have this thought, you see.
Do little sleeping monsters scream
Who dream
Of meeting me?

Max Fatchen

THE DAUGHTER OF THE FARRIER

The daughter of the farrier
Could find no one to marry her,
Because she said
She would not wed
A man who could not carry her.

The foolish girl was wrong enough,
And had to wait quite long enough;
For as she sat
She grew so fat
That nobody was strong enough.

FARRIER:
a blacksmith
who makes
horse shoes

HERE COMES THE BRIDE

Here comes the bride,
Sixty inches wide,
See how she wobbles,
From side to side.

Anon

THE SICK YOUNG DRAGON

'What can I do?' young dragon cried.
'Although I've simply tried and tried,
It doesn't matter how hard I blow,
I cannot get my fire to go!'

'Open your mouth!' his mother said.
'It's no wonder! Your throat's not red.
Your scales are cold. You must be ill.
I think you must have caught a chill.'

The doctor came. He looked and said,
'You'll need a day or two in bed.
Your temperature's down. No doubt
That's the reason your fire's gone out.

John Foster

'Just drink this petrol. Chew these nails
They'll help you warm up your scales.
Just take it easy. Watch TV,
You'll soon be right as rain, you'll see.'

Young dragon did as he was told
And soon his scales stopped feeling cold.
He sneezed some sparks. His face glowed bright.
He coughed and set the sheets alight.

'Oh dear' he cried. 'I've burnt the bed!'
'It doesn't matter,' his mother said.
'Those sheets were old. Go out and play.
Just watch where you breathe fire today!'

THEY LOOK LIKE LITTLE BASKETS

They look like little baskets,
Hanging up there in the tree.
I know that they are birds' nests,
But I think you will agree
That if their owners spent more time
And built a little roof,
Nests really would be warmer
And much more weather-proof.

Finola Akister

UNDER THE APPLE TREE

As I sat under the apple tree,
A birdie sent his love to me,
And as I wiped it from my eye,
I said, 'Thank goodness, cows can't fly.'

Anon

THERE WAS A CAT CALLED HOLLY

There was a cat called Holly,
She liked to wear bow ties.
Her favourite food was cheese on toast,
Spread thickly with dead flies.

When hunting in the darkest night,
She wore a clever disguise.
For fear of meeting face to face,
With something twice her size.

Now Holly's owner loved her lots,
Because she was so wise.
But Holly didn't know her plans,
To stuff her when she dies.

Sarah Ward

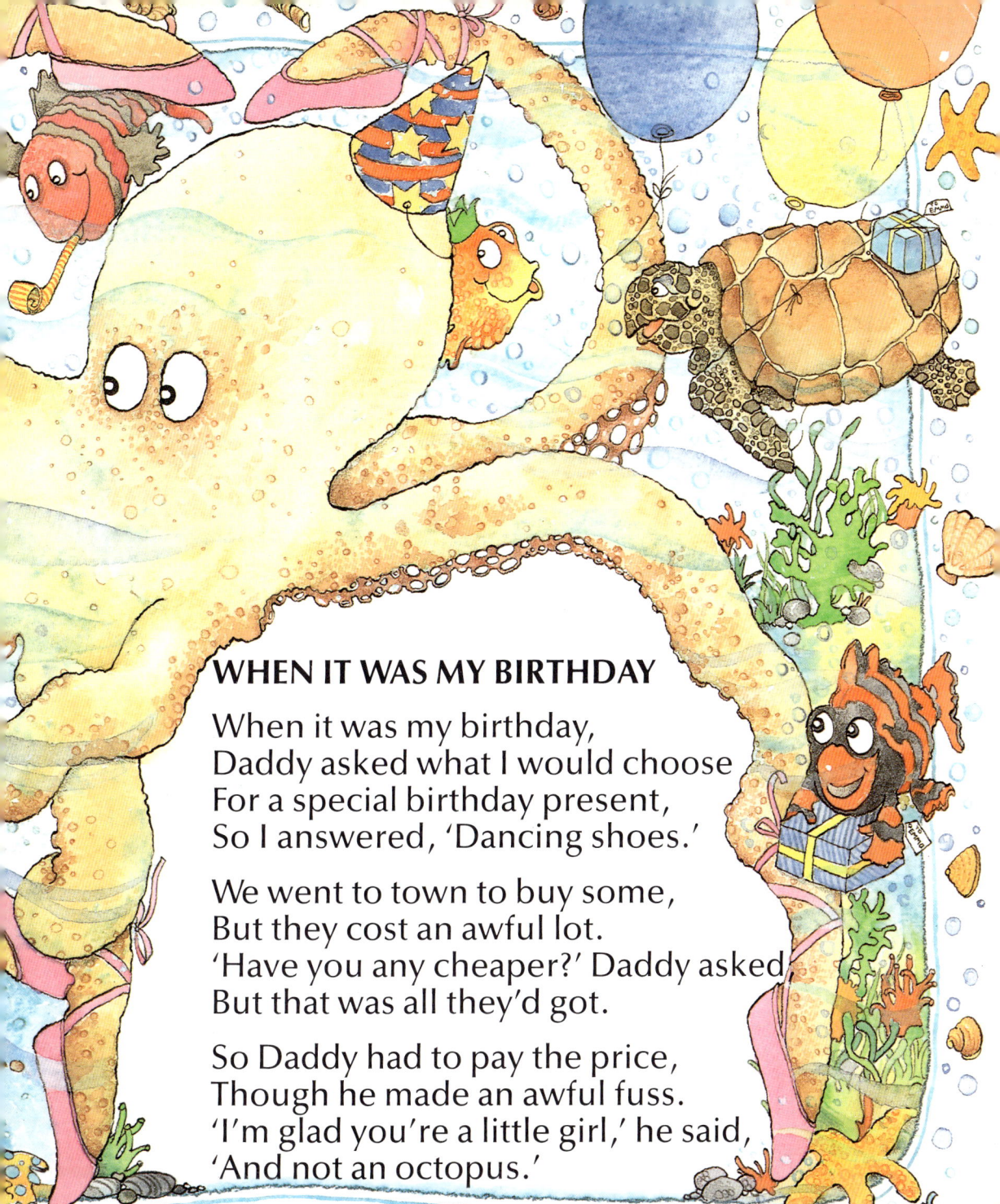

WHEN IT WAS MY BIRTHDAY

When it was my birthday,
Daddy asked what I would choose
For a special birthday present,
So I answered, 'Dancing shoes.'

We went to town to buy some,
But they cost an awful lot.
'Have you any cheaper?' Daddy asked,
But that was all they'd got.

So Daddy had to pay the price,
Though he made an awful fuss.
'I'm glad you're a little girl,' he said,
'And not an octopus.'

Finola Akister

AUNT SAMANTHA

Aunt Samantha woke one day
and sat up in her bed,
when a middle-sized rhinoceros
sat squarely on her head.

She did not seem the least put out,
was not at all annoyed;
in fact, as she addressed the beast,
she sounded overjoyed.

'I'm very glad you're up there,
though you've squashed my head quite flat,
for you've saved me all the botherment
of putting on my hat.'

Jack Prelutsky

PLAYING SAFE

It's perfectly safe to play cards with big cats,
To trick you they will not have plotted.
Lions and Tigers and Leopards are honest,
And Cheetahs invariably spotted.

cheat!

John Boon

Jack Sally Sophie Alex Tommy Kate Jerry Polly Rick

Laura Sandy Mervyn Sobena

MY CLASS OF TWENTY-THREE

In my class there are many,
A girl with pig tails her name's Jenny.
Sophie, Laura and Sandy are silly,
Alex, Jack and Ben pick on Billy.

Judy and Sobena giggle all day,
All the boys in my class, they love Kay.
Lily is pretty and thinks she's a star,
Polly is clever and is told will go far.

The twins are called Mervyn and Jerry Quinn,
Sally is tallest and Sarah is thin.
Tommy is good looking and a bit of a pose,
Rick fights a lot and has a scar on his nose.

Jeff and Ken are tough and chew gum,
Patrick is soft and always wants his mum.
I'm the last one in my class of twenty-three,
My name's Kate and I'm just me.

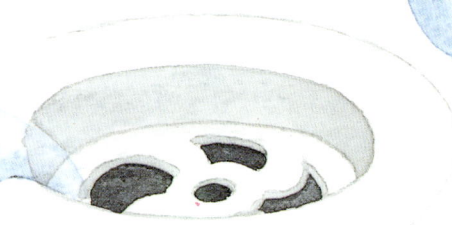

THE SPIDER IN DOC MARTENS

I saw a spider once,
Who was huge and really scary.
His elbows had web tattoos,
And his legs were very hairy.

With eyes like cherry tomatoes,
And Doc Martens on his feet.
Four pairs of boots, with laces tied,
All looking rather neat.

His mouth was big and wide,
With fangs like stalactites.
But when he smiled, I realised,
His bark's worse than his bite.

Harris Draw

HOW THE DINOSAUR GOT HERE

'Daddy, what's a dinosaur?'
Said my daughter Jane.
'The dinosaur was a giant beast
That will never be seen again.'

'Where did they all come from?'
'Now that I cannot say.'
And at this information
She turned and walked away

She must have thought about it,
For later that afternoon
She said to me, 'I know! I know!
They all came from the moon!'

'If that is true, my daughter,
Would you, pray, please tell
Exactly how they got here.'
She said, 'Of course – they fell!'

Spike Milligan

kadagic

THE WIZARD AND THE LIZARD

Once a wizard in a blizzard
Caught a lizard down a well.
First he took it, then he shook it,
Did he cook it? Time will tell.

How he stuttered as he muttered,
Till he spluttered out a spell.
Then, hey presto! Full of zest, o,
Have you guessed, O do not yell!

It was tragic that his magic
Word Kadagic wasn't right,
For the lizard in the blizzard.
Gave the wizard quite a fright.

It grew larger than a Rajah,
With a barge, a butt, a bite,
First it fizzled, till it grizzled,
Then it sizzled out of sight!

Colin West

THE RABBIT'S CHRISTMAS CAROL

I'm sick as a parrot,
I've lost me carrot,
I couldn't care less if it's
Christmas Day.

I'm sick as a parrot,
I've lost me carrot,
So get us a lettuce
Or...go away!

TO GRUMPY

Kit Wright

WHERE ARE YOU GOING?

Where are you going,
My little cat?

I am going to town,
To get me a hat.

What! A hat for a cat!
A cat get a hat!
Who ever saw a cat with a hat?

Anon

IN DAYS OF OLD

In days of old
The knights were bold
(Or so we're told).

And every day
Would dragons slay
(Or so they'd say),

And maidens fair
With flowery hair
Save from despair.

And armour clad,
With helm and flag,
Did joust and brag.

shush!

But knights today
No longer play
And dragons slay;

And maidens fair
Now take their share
Of toil and care.

Now in this land
The ladies stand
While men do sit
And sometimes knit;

'Tis plain to see
That chivalry
Is not to be.

R.A.W. COX

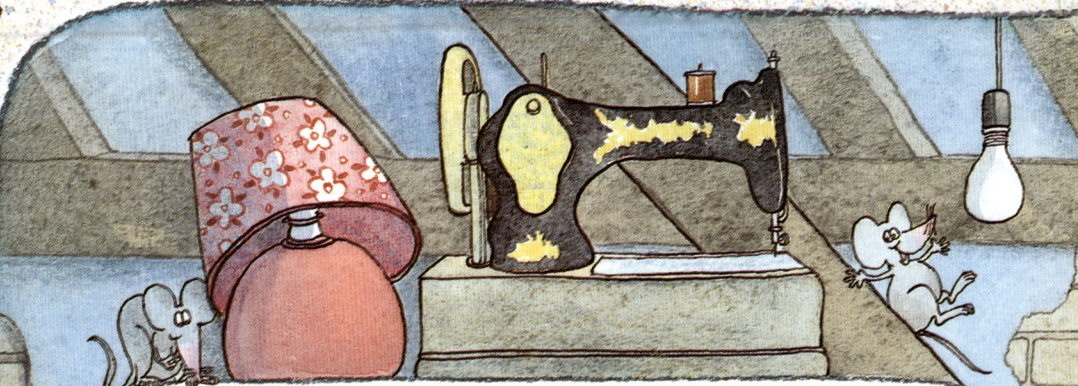

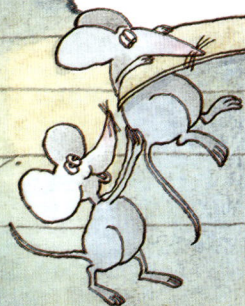

First published in Great Britain 1991
by Little Mammoth
an imprint of Mandarin Paperbacks
Michelin House, 81 Fulham Road,
London SW3 6RB

Mandarin is an imprint of the
Octopus Publishing Group

Illustrations copyright © 1991 Julie Park

ISBN 0 7497 0311 3

Printed in Great Britain by Scotprint Ltd.,
Musselburgh

Harris Draw

Max Fatchen

Jill Batterley

John Foster

Kit Wright

Colin West

Jack Prelutsky